A mother beaver and her young rest in the sunshine after a swim.

Busy Beavers

by M. Barbara Brownell

BOOKS FOR YOUNG EXPLORERS
NATIONAL GEOGRAPHIC SOCIETY

Beside a pond, a beaver snacks on tall grass and weeds.
On land, beavers find trees to use for making their homes,
called lodges. They build the lodges in deep water.
A beaver swims back and forth from its home to the land.

This beaver is busy building
a dam to hold water back
in a pond. Soon the water will be
deep and will be a safe place
for the beaver to build its lodge.

With its sharp front teeth,
the beaver cuts a branch in two.
A hard orange coating on the
teeth keeps them from chipping
as the beaver bites through wood.

In fall, a beaver works extra hard to get its lodge and dam ready for winter. It carries old grass and mud from the bottom of the pond and packs them into cracks between branches. Then it adds more branches. Underwater, the beaver pushes sticks into the lodge to make it strong. When it is finished, the lodge is big enough to hold a beaver family.

Lodge

Food pile

Dam

Dam

Canal

Soon, beavers cut
down most of the trees
by the water. Then
they go into the woods
for more trees.

Beavers have short legs
and cannot walk fast.
They need to stay near
water for safety.
So they dig a canal
from the pond to the
woods. They bring
logs back in the water.

On land, a beaver is always on the lookout for enemies.
This beaver has run into a bear cub that is just curious.

Whether a beaver is working or playing, it stays close to the water. If afraid, the beaver will dive in and swim away.

A beaver sniffs the air and listens. If it senses danger—perhaps a fox or a coyote—the beaver starts swimming and raises its tail in the air.

Suddenly—WHAP! The beaver slaps its tail against the water. The loud noise tells other beavers that danger is nearby. Then the beaver swims to its lodge.

Two beavers enter their
lodge underwater, through
a tunnel that runs from
the pond into the lodge.

Beavers swim very fast.
Their hind feet are webbed
like a duck's and help them
move through the water.
A beaver uses its
wide, flat tail to steer.

Beavers swim all year
around, even in icy water.
A layer of fat helps keep
them warm. Their fur is
very thick—and waterproof!

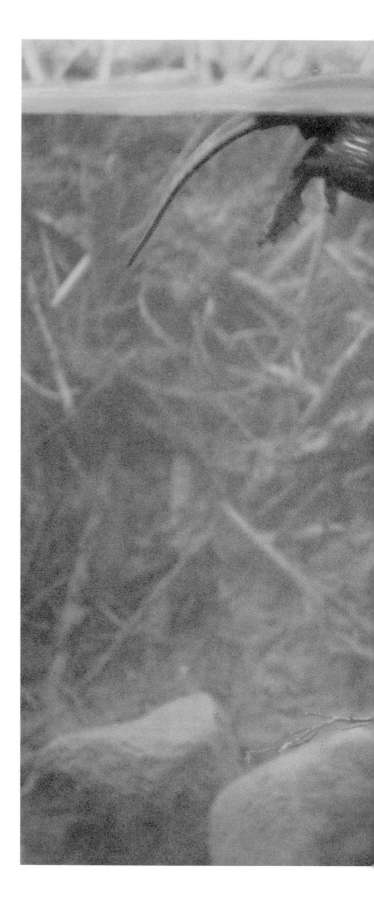

Inside the lodge, an adult beaver greets a baby that waits on a dry shelf above the water. The shelf is covered with twigs. There, a beaver family eats, plays, and rests.
The female usually gives birth to four or more babies. They are called kits. At first, the kits only drink their mother's milk. Soon, they eat grass, twigs, and bark, too.

Peek into a snow-covered lodge. Inside, a beaver family is warm and safe. The lodge is coated with mud that freezes and becomes as hard as rock. Enemies cannot break in.

Beavers stay busy all through the winter. When food runs low, adult beavers swim to an underwater food pile they built in the fall. The babies are born in late spring. In some places where beavers live, it may still be snowing when beavers are born.

If you see a lodge like this on a cold day, take a look around. You may see a beaver that has come out for a crunchy snack—a twig it found in the ice.

A newborn kit, smaller than your fist, gets a lot of attention. The mother nurses her kits on the shelf where they were born.

When it is five days old, the kit learns to swim. It waddles to the edge of the shelf and dives into the shallow pool below. PLOP! The kit can swim within a few hours.

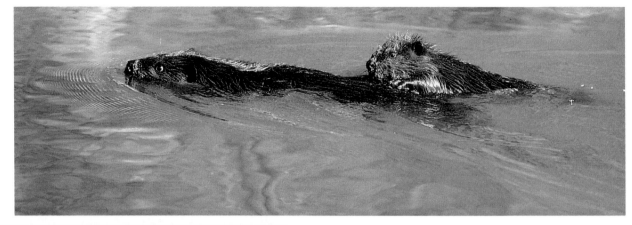

In late spring, the kits begin to swim outside the lodge. Their mother helps them. A tired kit may ride on its mother's back. Later, the mother may gently hold a kit in her mouth and push it to land. There, all the beavers rest in the sun.

Beavers often sunbathe. They may lie down, almost like sunbathers at the beach. But soon their tails and webbed feet begin to dry out, and they dive into the water for a cool swim.

A beaver has clear lids under its eyelids. Underwater, a beaver closes the clear lids, and it can see right through them.

PSSST . . . Is this mother sharing secrets with her babies? Maybe she is! Parents and their young talk to each other by rubbing noses and by making soft noises. Sometimes they call out to each other by whistling.

By the time a beaver is two years old, it is full grown.
Now it leaves its family to live on its own. It travels along
the bank of a river, a lake, or a pond. From time to time, it
may sniff the mud on the bank. A male beaver can tell from
the smell if a female is nearby, and a female knows if a male
has been there. If the two meet, they may become mates.

The mates swim off together. Can you guess what their first job will be? To look for a place to build a lodge so they can start their own family. The mates may stay together for life.

Published by

The National Geographic Society,
   Washington, D.C.
Gilbert M. Grosvenor,
   President and Chairman of the Board
Melvin M. Payne, Thomas W. McKnew,
   Chairmen Emeritus
Owen R. Anderson, *Executive Vice President*
Robert L. Breeden, *Senior Vice President,*
   Publications and Educational Media

Prepared by

The Special Publications
   and School Services Division
Donald J. Crump, *Director*
Philip B. Silcott, *Associate Director*
Bonnie S. Lawrence, *Assistant Director*

Staff for this book

Jane H. Buxton, *Managing Editor*
Charles M. Kogod, *Illustrations Editor*
Jody Bolt, *Art Director*
Gregory A. McGruder, *Researcher*
Barbara Gibson, *Artist*
Sharon Kocsis Berry, *Illustrations Assistant*
Susan A. Bender, Marisa J. Farabelli, Kaylene Kahler,
   Sandra F. Lotterman, Eliza C. Morton, Dru McLoud
Stancampiano, *Staff Assistants*

Engraving, Printing, and Product Manufacture

George V. White, *Director, Manufacturing*
   and Quality Management
Vincent P. Ryan, *Manager, Manufacturing*
   and Quality Management
David V. Showers, *Production Manager*
Kathleen M. Cirucci, *Production Project Manager*
Carol R. Curtis, *Senior Production Staff Assistant*

Consultants

Dr. Richard W. Coles, Tyson Research Center, Washington
   University, and Dr. Gerald Svendsen, Ohio University,
   Scientific Consultants
Dr. Ine N. Noe, *Educational Consultant*
Dr. Lynda Bush, *Reading Consultant*

Illustrations Credits

Tom and Pat Leeson (cover, 6 upper, 6-7, 13 upper);
Wolfgang Bayer Productions (1, 24 upper, 24 center, 25, 28-29);
Mark Newman/WEST STOCK (2-3); François Gohier/PHOTO
RESEARCHERS (3 lower); Leonard Lee Rue III (4-5, 6 lower);
Gary Milburn/TOM STACK & ASSOCIATES (6 center);
Jen & Des Bartlett (10-11, 16, 17, 22 lower, 22-23, 24 lower, 26-27,
31 lower); John W. Warden (12); Stephen J. Krasemann/
DRK PHOTO (13 lower); Jim Brandenburg (14-15);
Stephen J. Krasemann/NATIONAL AUDUBON SOCIETY
COLLECTION, PHOTO RESEARCHERS (20); Diana Stratton/
TOM STACK & ASSOCIATES (21); Wolfgang Bayer/BRUCE
COLEMAN INC (22 upper); ANIMALS ANIMALS/Ray Richardson
(30-31); Dennis W. Schmidt/VALAN PHOTOS (32).

Library of Congress ℂℙ Data

Brownell, M. Barbara.
   Busy beavers.
   (Books for young explorers)
   Bibliography: p.
   Summary: Photographs and text introduce the physical
characteristics and habits of the beaver.
   1. Beavers—Juvenile literature.   [1. Beavers   I. Title.
II. Series.
QL737.R632B76   1988   599.32′32   88-19703
ISBN 0-87044-740-8 (regular edition)
ISBN 0-87044-745-9 (library edition)

It's snacktime!
A beaver gnaws a
fallen birch tree.

Cover: Hard at
work, a beaver
keeps its balance
by propping itself
up with its tail.

MORE ABOUT Busy Beavers

This tree, about a foot and a half in diameter, may have taken the beaver several nights to cut down. To gnaw a tree, a beaver stands upright and balances on its tail. Scientists do not know why beavers often fail to gnaw all the way through (right).

Busy beavers live in areas with forests and water in North America, Europe, and Asia. They make their homes in lakes, ponds, and rivers. The animals are shy, and the casual visitor might not see them. But if you know what to look for, you might spot them.

Take a walk with your child along a pond, a stream, or a canal, searching for signs of beaver activity. Is the water backed up behind a dam of sticks and mud (8-9)?* Do you see a dome-shaped mound made of the same materials (6-7, 18-19, 20)? Are there pointed tree stumps nearby?

*Numbers in parentheses refer to pages in *Busy Beavers*.

A beaver sometimes abandons a tree before felling it. Scientists don't know why. If you see a tree like the one at right, help your child imagine what happened. One first grader wrote this story:

"The beaver was starting to chop wood. He saw a squirrel coming down the tree, so he didn't get quite finished. Then he started another hole in the tree. And the squirrel was getting closer, so the beaver only got three-quarters of it down. And the squirrel was getting so close and the beaver was so afraid, he ran home to his lodge."

Beavers belong to the animal order Rodentia, the mammals that gnaw. This order includes squirrels, mice, and rats, among others, and has far more members than any other order of mammals. Rodents have continuously growing front teeth, which they keep trimmed by gnawing and gnashing.

Larger than most rodents, a beaver may grow to four feet in length, including tail, and may weigh as much as 80 pounds. Its front teeth may grow an inch long on top and two inches on the bottom.

The front teeth are powerful tools. Their hard orange coating makes them strong. Constant gnawing keeps them sharp. When it gnaws (8-9, 32), a beaver grips the wood with its upper teeth. Shoving its lower jaw forward, the beaver chisels with the lower teeth. It avoids swallowing chips by closing flaps of skin behind the front teeth. When the beaver gnaws wood underwater, the flaps close out water as well as wood.

Along a quiet stream, beavers cut down trees—usually alder, willow, and aspen. Next, they gnaw the trees into pieces, which they roll or drag to their damsite. There they jam sticks into the streambed and anchor them with rocks. On this foundation, they pile up branches, leaves, and roots. They may even add bottles or car tires. Finally, they coat the dam with mud from the streambed (6), making it watertight. As the dam grows, a pond forms behind it.

In the pond, beavers build their lodge. Its dome rises above the water. From underwater, they tunnel into the mound and hollow out a living area (18-19). Beavers leave spaces between sticks in the roof that serve as air vents.

A beaver always builds a dam, creating a pond, before building a lodge. The beaver must know the level of the pond so it can hollow out a living space above the water. It must be sure the pond is deep enough to fill the lodge entrances with water and block out enemies.

Some beavers live along lakes or by swift rivers that cannot be dammed. Without a deep pond, the beavers cannot build a lodge. So they tunnel from underwater up into the bank. There they dig dens.

On land, beavers are vulnerable to enemies because they are slow runners. Sometimes they dig tunnels between the water and the woods. When danger threatens, they slip down the entrance hole.

As you explore, you may come across small cone-shaped piles of mud every few feet. These are signposts left by a young beaver searching for a mate. At the age of two, a beaver leaves its family. Some beavers will then look for a mate. They travel along a bank, piling up mud. With a few drops of castoreum, a substance released from internal pouches near the base of their tails, they mark the mud with their scent. A male may detect a female's scent and follow the mud piles until he finds her. Similarly, a female may find a male.

To see a beaver, try visiting the water at sunset, when most beavers come out to work. You may not see one at first. Then suddenly you may hear a SLAP! as its tail hits the water. That is the signal that danger is near. *You* are the danger. You may turn around just in time to see the beaver swim to safety (3).

As it dives, the beaver clamps shut its nostrils and ears (26-27). It closes the transparent membranes under its eyelids. Then it zips along at 5 miles an hour. Strong lungs enable

a beaver to swim underwater for 15 minutes—and for half a mile. It swims in warm or icy water. It has a split claw on each hind foot, which it uses to comb oil through its fur (28-29). The oil, secreted from glands, makes the coat waterproof.

Fascinating as the beaver is, it is considered a nuisance by some people. Beavers fell valuable trees for their lodges and dams, and the ponds they create flood the surrounding land. Many conservationists, however, believe that the beaver helps support a cycle of nature. A beaver pond creates a haven for fish, water birds, and other animals. Rich soil builds up in the pond, rather than washing downstream. Years after the beavers have left, new plants grow out of this soil. Eventually, a new forest may thrive there.

At the turn of the century, beavers were nearly extinct. Most had been killed off for their rich fur. Since then, programs in the United States and Canada have been reintroducing the beaver into national forests. Today, North America has more beavers than any other continent. That means there are plenty of places for you and your child to look for—and enjoy—them.

ADDITIONAL READING

Animal Architects, (Washington, D. C., National Geographic Society, 1981). Ages 8 and up.

Animals of the Ponds and Streams, by Julie Becker. (St. Paul, Minn., EMC Corp., 1977). Ages 8 and up.

Beaver at Long Pond, by William T. George and Lindsay Barrett George. (New York, Greenwillow Books, 1988). Ages 5 and up.

Beavers, by James Poling. (New York, Franklin Watts, Inc., 1975). Ages 8 and up.